Sam's Bike

Written by Leonie Bennett
Illustrated by Julie Park

Rosie had a new bike.

Tilak had a new bike . . .

and Adam had a new bike.

Sam had Adam's old bike.

Rosie's mum gave her a push.

Tilak's dad gave him a push.

Sam's mum was busy.
Sam's dad was busy . . .

but Adam gave him a push.

Rosie's mum was tired.

Tilak's dad was tired.

But Adam went on pushing and pushing and pushing until ...

Sam could ride his bike!